The Soul of Korean Architecture

Asem Al-Wasli

Fuad Al-Qrize

Maher Asaad Baker

Softcover: 978-3-384-18766-6

Hardcover: 978-3-384-18767-3

eBook: 978-3-384-18768-0

Large print: 978-3-384-18769-7

Contents

Introduction

The architectural accomplishments of ancient Korea are a testament to the innovative spirit, technical sophistication, and aesthetic sensibilities of its people. Through careful study, we can develop a profound respect for those who came before us, and gain insight into how their built environments both shaped, and were shaped by the social, political, and spiritual dimensions of Korean civilization.

The earliest surviving examples of constructed shelters in the Korean peninsula date back to Neolithic settlements of around 8000 BC, during the Jeulmun Pottery Period. These comprised simple pit dwellings dug into the ground, sometimes lined with stone, with thatched sod or woven reed roofs. By 1500 BC in the Bronze Age, raised architecture had emerged involving post-and-beam wooden structures placed directly on the earth, as evidenced by archaeological sites. Climate and topographical conditions on the Korean peninsula incentivized the development of efficient load-bearing wood joinery that could withstand harsh winters and summer monsoon rains.

From the 3rd century BC Gojoseon period to the 1st century AD, palace complexes, and tomb structures reflected increasing social hierarchy, and ritual importance of burial rites. Earthen walls circled cities, and flagstone-paved roads connected settlements, pointing to early urban planning. Goguryeo period architecture from the 1st century BC to the 7th century AD demonstrated geometric symmetry, woodwork mastery, and advanced tiled roofing. Stately mud-wall fortress-cities were raised, some featuring inner and outer citadels with protective moats, and sentry towers - manifestations of a sophisticated militaristic culture.

Goguryeo's architectural zenith was seen in Anak Tomb No. 3, a pyramidal five-chamber burial structure faced with neatly cut stone blocks. Interior painted frescoes hint at the refinement of concurrent wooden buildings, though none survive intact today. Raised wood, and thatch domestic housing became standardized during Silla (57 BC-935 AD), and Balhae (691-926 AD) periods, with distinct gabled, and hipped saddleback roof styles developing. Socioeconomic specialization and populations supported urbanization, establishing a durable foundation for future Korean architectural forms.

The unified Goryeo Dynasty built extensively upon earlier traditions while establishing several formative conventions that would persist into the Joseon era. Buddhism gained widespread patronage, reflected in grand sanctuaries like the 11th-century Five-Story Stone Pagoda, and Seokguram Grotto, technical masterworks showcasing refined masonry, tiled roofs, and woodwork sculptural detail. Stone became important for pagoda substructures, allowing taller multistory designs, though buildings themselves remained principally of wood joints, tiles, and plaster.

Distinctive architectural elements emerged such as jeonji bul, curved gable extensions supported by decorated brackets above secondary eaves. Multi-room, one-story geomun (servant quarters) flanked larger two-story oge (main residences) in yangban aristocrat homes. Palace complexes expanded with raised wooden halls, bridges, and pavilions set among landscaped gardens connected by walkways - early examples of elegant scholastic compounds integrated with nature that would later characterize Korean nobility residences.

Urban planning principles coalesced around walled cities containing jangseong fortress towers, administrative buildings, and residential quarters centered on main boulevards.

Standardized hanok wooden domestic architecture evolved, optimized for cold winters yet ventilation in summer, featuring raised wooden floorboards, heated ondol underfloor systems, warm roofs with extended eaves, sliding screens, and walls allowing flexible indoor-outdoor living. These designs maximized livable space within modest footprints, becoming iconic of traditional Korean residential culture.

During its 500-year reign, the Joseon Dynasty saw immense cultural, and technological progress alongside socio-political stability, allowing Korean architecture, and planning to fully mature. Confucian philosophy guided the harmonious siting of palaces, shrines, and yangban elites' villages concerning natural landscapes. Consolidated design standards appeared, such as the regulated architectural mapping (gyecheop) system for public works including palace complexes, and government offices in cities.

Palaces expanded under a standard gyeongcheong plan - symmetrical axes, ceremonial archways, paved main boulevards, and two-story halls faced with a polished stone or wooden walls enclosing inner walled courtyards. The apogee, Gyeongbokgung Palace, was meticulously erected in the 15th century with tall blue-tiled hip-and-gable roofs atop gray stone walls, and platforms. Finer outdoor, and indoor architectural elements of carved, and painted wooden embellishments reached stunning sophistication.

Donglimmun and Donuimun ceremonial gates emerged as defining images of palace entrances crowned by triple-gabled hip-and-gable roofs supported by large decorative brackets, exemplifying Korean mastery over complex curved architectural wooden members. Elsewhere, fortress towns like Hwaseong proclaimed progressive late 18th-century military architecture and landscaping principles.

The yangban scholar-official class constructed elegant yet understated scholar's retreats (seowon) blending study halls, and landscaped surroundings that fostered intellectual, and spiritual pursuits. Commoner residential areas in walled cities contained densely packed yet meticulously ordered hanoks adapted to small lots. Rural farm villages featured thatch-roofed homes encircled by raised earthen mounds, and ridges serving defensive-practical functions.

Despite periods of fragmentation and foreign oppression, traditional Korean architectural forms proved remarkably persistent, and adaptive. Though battered by modernization campaigns of the 20th century, important elements survive today in reconstructed heritage sites, continuing cultural functions, and modified living architectural styles. Perhaps above all, hanok homes remain iconic globally recognized symbols of the refined yet pragmatic adaptations evolved over millennia by the resilient Korean people and their building traditions.

By studying traditional Korean architecture's evolutionary origins, and innovations across dynasties, we can appreciate the ingenuity, technical sophistication, and aesthetic sensibilities embedded within its indigenous cultural vocabulary of forms. These evolved solutions reflected intimate relationships Koreans cultivated with place, climate, available materials, societal structures, and spiritual dimensions of lived experience. A heritage of adaptive innovation for maximizing livable space, mitigating harsh weather, defending settlements, and crafting refined interior-exterior living integration merits renewed respect, and understanding across borders in our increasingly interconnected world.

Traditional Korean architecture manifested a deeply respectful relationship with the natural landscape. For centuries, it has blended structures seamlessly into their environments through the use of indigenous materials, awareness of topography, and climate considerations, and emphasis on hierarchical positioning reflecting Confucian cosmic order. Palaces, shrines, scholar's retreats, and villages were carefully sited, and oriented according to feng shui principles aligning with mountain, and water flows. Buildings' scaled incorporation of outer ridges, terraces, and inner landscaped courtyards fostered a centered mindset attuned to seasonal changes and celestial rhythms.

This organic integration went hand in hand with pragmatic measures, from raised foundations preventing flooding to warm roofs with extended eaves shielding harsh winds, and rain. Window placement and hewn ventilation gaps maximized natural lighting, and airflow according to thermal dynamics. The resulting architectural works nestled snugly into scenery in relationship rather than rivalry with nature, whose balanced energies, and aesthetic scenes they respectfully complemented rather than dominated. This Confucian-inspired view of humans as stewards living in partnership rather than mastery over landscapes has profoundly shaped Korea's cultural identity, and connection to place.

Traditional residential hanok housing demonstrated architectural intelligence finely calibrated to topography while cultivating close-knit communities supported by adjacent agricultural, and administrative quarters. Their meticulous arrangement and division of living spaces fused interior-exterior realms, fluidly dissolving barriers between families, and neighbors through shared walkways, courtyards, and village compounds oriented along mountain spines. This community living facilitated cooperation, neighborhood bonds, and mutual assistance essential for coping with climatic adversity, upholding societal cohesion, and order through all strata of society from palaces to farming hamlets.

Throughout Korean history, spiritual ideas have powerfully motivated architectural innovations and the proliferation of related artistic works. Buddhism in particular stimulated technical developments like stone pagoda construction, and the refinement of delicate sculptural woodwork embellishing prayer halls, and shrines from the Goryeo era onward. Religious sites blended with nature along rivers, and mountains formed focal nodes anchoring surrounding village life. Grand palace Buddhist sanctuaries like Beopjusa served as loci where royalty, clergy, and commoners congregated, and reinforced a shared cultural foundation. Their architectural magnificence and ornamental details metaphorically lifting the soul heavenward portrayed an achievement of human-divine union through virtuous refinement of both physical structures and interior lives.

Confucian philosophy also shaped architectural forms, and spatial flows, from the ordered layouts of palaces, and scholar's villages to symmetrical feng shui siting relative to geographic features. Emphasis was placed on hierarchical yet balanced relationships between physical components, and occupants reflecting harmonious social interconnectedness. Rectilinear precedence of main halls, central axes, and partitioning of family versus scholarly spaces using delicate wood screens were manifestations of an ethical system tying individual cultivation to upholding stable communal bonds. Their understated refinement signified moderation, and emphasis on inner virtues over outward show, communicating Confucian priorities through the language of structure, materials, and flow of daily routines.

Traditional Korean architectural aesthetics synthesized pragmatism, spirituality, and conceptions of order into a sophisticated formal vocabulary recognizable worldwide as a cultural symbol. Distinct features included tall graceful tiled roofs culminating in swooping gracefully extended eaves supported by decorative bracketry, stone fortress walls, and platforms, ornate wooden embellishments like carved dragon-shaped ridgelines, and floral motifs. composed forms projected elegant simplicity elevating function through studied balance of solids, and voids.

Intricate wood joinery and painting traditions generated interior dividers, doors, and exposed beamwork of stunning sculptural complexity, and visual rhythm equaling any contemporaneous art form. Careful proportions, and repetition of modular design elements across scales produced unity within variety maintaining coherence from grand palace complexes down to individual building components. Textural contrasts of polished stone, rough-hewn wood, glazed roof tiles, and neat plaster complemented cleanlined compositions, while bright interior colors, and gardens further animated strict symmetrical plans.

These refined aesthetic sensibilities have left an indelible mark on notions of beauty globally, from Zen rock gardens to modern architecture. They communicate simultaneously pragmatic livability, metaphorical spiritual ideals, and uniquely Korean artistic spirit through mastery of materials dedicated to craft over empty materialism. Their hereditary cumulative perfection symbolized a civilization's patience, communal work ethic, and artistic striving for harmony between man, and nature inbuilt into the humblest domestic structures.

Ultimately, the widespread influence of Korean architectural forms stemmed from their capacity to physically shape social structures, and cultural mindsets over generations. Traditional housing stock reinforced boundaries between gendered family roles yet permeable social divisions, with women inhabiting inner kitchen spaces, and men outer courtyards according protocol. Standardization of hanok formats stabilized the population by optimizing population densities within walled villages, and cities.

Their ordered self-contained socio-functional zoning supported evolving hierarchical systems from clan-based to Confucian bureaucratic orders. Fortress-like construction provided psychological as well as practical defense mechanisms stabilizing polities. Grand palatial complexes communicated sovereignty and maintained ritual functions anchoring centralized governments for centuries. Scholar-official residential compounds cultivated literati social bonds, and philosophical study.

Through accumulated iterations, these structured environments naturalized behaviors, values, and conceptual frameworks at both individual and collective levels. They became internalized as taken-for-gratenormative blueprints underpinning progressive aspects of Korean identity even amid rapid modernization. Heritage sites, ongoing architectural revival movements, and exported influence globally signify the profound, and persistent cultural impacts sedimented by traditional architectural forms that stabilized a civilization through integration of art, ethics, and lived experience over millennia.

Traditional Korean architecture manifested a uniquely refined artistic language alloying pragmatic function, spiritual philosophies, and aesthetic ideals into built forms that shaped social development and propagated a distinct cultural identity. By understanding architecture's legacy of facilitating community living, upholding shared symbolic meanings, and optimizing infrastructure to reinforce stabilizing cultural patterns, one gains newfound respect for its immense role in guiding Korean civilization's evolutionary path. Its influence illuminates aspects of what allowed continuity, and progress amid turbulent changes, contributing lessons applicable far beyond any single region or era.

Traditional Korean Architecture

When examining a civilization's artistic accomplishments, profound insight can be gained into the character of its culture, values, and social structures. In Korea, no single architectural form carries more symbolic meaning than the traditional Hanok house. For centuries, the Hanok evolved as a uniquely refined structure calibrating pragmatic function, and aesthetic beauty to reflect Confucian socio-cultural ideals. Despite modernization efforts obliterating much of the housing stock, revival movements recognize Hanok architecture's vital role in defining Korean identity. While architectural styles inevitably adapt across eras, certain abiding core architectural, and philosophical principles underlying Hanok design merit closer analysis for their contributions to shaping Korean society.

The earliest raised Hanok structures emerged in the Goryeo Dynasty from the 10th century AD, with design principles maturing fully under the Joseon Dynasty. Hanoks comprised wooden frames constructed without nails using intricate mortise-and-tenon joinery, and mud-plastered walls allowing natural airflow and insulation against harsh climates. Raised wooden foundations elevated living spaces while symmetrically partitioning family and scholarly activities.

Central features included ondol underfloor heating systems circulating warm air, warm tiled hipped roofs with deep overhanging eaves, sturdy red or blue-gray roof tiles, sliding wood-frame, and paper-paned doors, and windows optimized for seasons. Spatial organization focused on open yet semi-enclosed interior courtyards bringing light and air into nested rooms. Established modular design standards stabilized housing formats across social classes as populations grew within walled cities.

The enduring Hanok blueprint delicately balanced function, aesthetic appeal, and Confucian social symbolism to define an entire civilization's residential culture for over a millennium with pragmatism, and artistic beauty intrinsically interwoven. Its replicated ubiquity stabilized Korean life through cooperative urban infrastructural planning underscoring shared values amid natural, and political upheavals.

Beyond utilitarian shelter, Hanok spatial organization projected Confucian notions of family hierarchy, gender roles, and virtue. An outer sarangchae zone contained men's quarters, and reception areas, while inner anchae held women's kitchens, and living spaces following propriety separating public, and private realms. Subtle design variations distinguished yangban elite from commoners' dwellings, though all reinforced patriarchal order through differentiated yet codependent familial roles.

Compound structures aggregated multiple generations under one roof, reinforcing multigenerational bonds, and mutual support systems. Standardizing modules stabilized hyper-dense urban planning, maximizing populations supported within walled community frameworks. Just as architectural forms conditioned behavioral patterns, Confucian social patterns found physical representation stabilizing mindsets. Harmonizing necessity, and cultural psychology, Hanoks served as a collective anchor shaping Korean identity.

Beyond material form alone, Hanoks embodied a spiritual consciousness attuned to ancestral veneration, harmony with nature, and the quest for perfection through patience. Open woodwork framing allowed connection to ancestral spirits, and nature's flowing vital energies according to feng shui principles in siting, and layout. Delicate craftsmanship symbolized respect for passed generations through multi-year construction processes nurturing community bonds.

Architectural refinements through small consecutive adjustments, humble materials meticulously prepared, and placed all suggested dedication to cultivation of virtue through imperceptible incremental betterment – ideals Confucianism, and Buddhism shared. Mud walls 'breathed', adaptively separating without dividing space according to climatic dictates like flowing water symbolizing primordial qi energy. Through buildings' symbiotic integration with human, natural, and celestial rhythms, Hanoks uplifted spirit while anchoring its craftspeople, and inhabitants in timelessness.

Early twentieth century modernization campaigns nearly eradicated Korea's Hanok housing stock, yet reconstruction efforts reveal their artistic sophistication equaling any contemporaneous art form. Geometrically balanced layouts allowed the proportionate unfolding of exquisite woodcraft traditions through curved bracketry, mural paintings, latticed bamboo screens, and detailed carvings animating clean architectural lines. Warm red roof tiles, gray stonework, and white plaster complemented rich interior hues, establishing a palette now globally associated with Korean aesthetics.

Hanoks' refined simplicity, and functional beauty particularly influenced modernist, and contemporary Japanese architecture through shared cultural exchange. Their modulated compositions integrate rigor, and restraint through studied cadences of solid wood, and space-channeled meditative, and poetic sensibilities. Experiencing lived Hanok spaces heightens appreciation for architectural art elevated to enhance daily life through ordered placement of natural textures. These influences spread worldwide, imprinting design principles that dignified humble beginnings through artistic attainment dedicated to life's realities.

Though contemporary lifestyles rendered Hanoks obsolete, preservation movements recognize their invaluable cultural legacy necessitating revival. Reconstructed heritage sites like Hanok Village in Seoul attract tourists to experience living history. Citizens participate actively in annual Llayoetnal, cooperative rebuilding ceremonies honoring ancestral construction techniques.

Private initiatives couple traditional designs with modern conveniences to pass living architectural traditions to new generations. Municipal supportive policies incentivize Hanok restoration projects combining historic authenticity with eco-friendly materials. Their intimate scaled, human proportions contradict impersonal ubiquitous high-rises, signaling desire for rootedness, and balanced development.

As globalization homogenizes cultures, Hanoks symbolize living continuity tying Koreans to homeland through generations who labored crafting these landmark structures. Just as Confucianism views architecture as embodiment of virtue manifesting over extended time, Hanoks' revitalization ensures cultural psychology survives modern upheavals bypassing ephemeral fashions. Their preservation sustains an entire civilization's artistic, and philosophical heritage in built form.

Traditional Hanok residential architecture represents far more than utilitarian shelter—it served as a physical carrier encoding Korea's spiritual principles, social structures, and artistic refinement over centuries into its woven wood grains, and fired clay. Despite modern changes, Hanoks remain a defining national symbol through ongoing revival maintaining architectural forms that shaped Korean identity by integrating necessity, beauty, and collective psychology into the humblest domestic space. Their cultural significance illuminates architecture's capacity to stabilize civilizations by physically embedding shared values across eras.

The earliest surviving royal residences date to the Three Kingdoms Period, such as 5th century AD Goguryeo's Anapji palace ruins featuring earthen walls, stone foundations, and wooden buildings. Under unified Silla, and Balhae, standardized one-story palace frameworks emerged set against mountain backdrops according to feng shui geomantic principles aligning spiritually with nature, and cosmological patterns. Basic layouts organized facilities into inner, and outer zones with central audience halls, and residences surrounded by secondary structures within wood-fenced enclosures.

The Goryeo period saw construction of new palace cities and the expansion of precedents established by earlier kingdoms. Grander two-story wooden architecture reflected increasing refinement, and technical prowess in woodworking, and tiled roofing. The 12th century Gaegyeong Palace exemplified architectural flowering under aristocratic Song Dynasty cultural influences from China. Its towering blue-green tiled hip-and-gable roofs soaring above white walls left architectural imprints carried through subsequent eras. Advancing stone masonry allowed taller seven-story pagodas integrating painted wooden interiors depicting Buddhist cosmology with exteriors' geometric symmetry.

During 500 years of stability under the Joseon, Korea's indigenous architectural traditions fully matured. Confucian core values of order, hierarchy, and balance between man, and nature found expression in gyeongcheong palace standardization. Grand complexes systematically unfolded along symmetrical orthogonal axes designed according to geomantic principles. Elaborating Goryeo precedents, palaces comprised paved main boulevards, elaborate wooden halls, and pavilions joined by covered walkways within walled inner compounds, and ceremonial outer zones defined by imposing guardian statues, arched gateways, and arched bridges crossing lotus ponds.

Gyeongbokgung Palace built during the 1400s represented its architectural, and symbolic apex, housing the royal residence until the Japanese invasion of 1592. Its meticulous construction solidified architectural codification achieved after centuries of incremental refinement. Stone bases, and reinforced earthen platforms carefully leveled the site. Behind perimeter walls, and ceremonial gates rose the two-story Daejojeon, and Seokjajeon halls where kings addressed officials, and subjects, faced by polished stone, and carved wooden detailing of unprecedented sophistication.

Interiors featured ornate artwork, furnishings, and murals while courtyards connected secondary structures. Visual sequences deliberately unfolding space, color, and symbolic programs oriented inhabitants within the ordered Confucian-based cosmos. No expense was spared to craft this landmark communicating sovereignty through architectural perfection intimately linked to rulership according to dynastic political philosophy. Gyeongbokgung's model endured through centuries with variations defining royal complexes country-wide.

Despite invasions, fires, and modernization, architectural styles established by Korean palaces persevered through reconstructed heritage sites. Chancellery sites like Deoksugung integrate traditional elegance with modern conveniences to preserve living culture. Changdeokgung's Secret Garden, and lesser palace Hwaseong in Suwon exemplify how harmonizing structural hierarchy with nature reflected Confucian-Daoist balance. Materials evolved to stone, while modular woodworking styles influenced global timberwork.

Formally, hip-and-gable tiled roofs supported by ornate bracketry remain immediately recognizable architectural symbols. Ceremonial gateways framed approaches to inner realms through regulated spatial progression. Consistent adherence to rigorous orthogonal layouts oriented inhabitants ritually within landscapes despite political upheavals. These conventions dignified occupants through orderly placement integrating aesthetics with virtuous governance according to dynastic political philosophies inextricably intertwining leadership and architectural forms.

Traditional Korean palaces represented pinnacles of indigenous cultural, and artistic accomplishments through centuries of refinement. Beyond utilitarian functions, their meticulously programmed architectural forms served symbolic roles upholding stable dynastic rule by physical embodiment of Confucian socio-political philosophies. Spatial layouts and formal conventions communicated ideals of hierarchical yet balanced relations between humans, governance structures, and the natural world according to geomantic principles. Reconstruction efforts preserve this heritage, invaluable for gaining deeper understanding into how architectural forms shaped Korean identity, and national character by encoding its highest cultural, and political values into its grandest landmark buildings.

Korean temple architecture is characterized by its simplicity, harmony, and seamless integration with nature. Unlike the grandiose, and ornate structures prevalent in other parts of the world, Korean temples exude a serene elegance, embodying the principles of balance, and moderation. This aesthetic ethos, known as 'pungsu' or geomancy, emphasizes the harmonious coexistence of humans, and nature, a philosophy deeply ingrained in Korean culture.

A typical Korean temple complex comprises several buildings arranged in a symmetrical layout. The main hall, or 'Daeungjeon', houses the primary deity, and is the focal point of the complex. This hall is flanked by subsidiary halls, lecture halls, dormitories, and a bell pavilion, all arranged in a precise order reflecting their hierarchical importance.

The 'Dancheong', or the vibrant paintwork adorning the temple buildings, is a distinctive feature of Korean temple architecture. These intricate designs, executed in a palette of five primary colors, serve both aesthetic and symbolic purposes. They are believed to ward off evil spirits and represent various cosmological elements.

Beyond its aesthetic appeal, Korean temple architecture holds deep spiritual significance. The temple complex is designed to facilitate a journey towards enlightenment, with each building representing a stage in this spiritual quest. The path leading to the main hall, often lined with stone lanterns, and pagodas, symbolizes the path of righteousness, guiding devotees towards the ultimate truth.

Despite the ravages of time and foreign invasions, many Korean temples have survived, bearing witness to the nation's rich architectural heritage. The preservation of these structures is a testament to Korea's reverence for its past, and its commitment to safeguarding its cultural legacy.

However, Korean temple architecture is not a static entity. It has evolved over the centuries, incorporating new elements, and adapting to changing circumstances. This dynamic interplay of tradition and innovation is evident in contemporary temple architecture, which combines age-old principles with modern aesthetics, and construction techniques.

Traditional Korean temple architecture is a profound manifestation of the nation's spiritual ethos and cultural identity. It embodies a philosophy of harmony, balance, and coexistence with nature, offering a unique perspective on the human condition, and our place in the universe. As we navigate the complexities of the modern world, these timeless wisdoms encapsulated in stone, and wood continue to resonate, reminding us of the enduring power of tradition, and the transformative potential of spirituality.

The Folk Village architecture is a living museum that showcases the traditional way of life in rural Korea. The village is carefully designed to replicate the architectural styles, layout, and environment of a typical Korean village from centuries ago. Buildings are constructed using locally sourced materials such as wood, clay, and straw, and are built in accordance with traditional Korean architectural principles. Each building serves a specific function, whether it be a residence, a workshop, or a communal space, with careful attention to detail in terms of layout, orientation, and design.

One of the most striking features of traditional Korean architecture is its emphasis on harmony with nature. Buildings are designed to blend seamlessly with the natural environment, utilizing elements such as courtyards, gardens, and natural lighting to create a sense of balance, and tranquility. The use of natural materials such as wood, and clay helps to regulate temperature, humidity, and air circulation, creating a comfortable, and sustainable living environment. Traditional Korean architecture also incorporates elements of Feng Shui, with careful consideration given to the orientation of buildings, placement of doors, and windows, and use of colors, and symbols to promote positive energy flow and enhance well-being.

In terms of design, and aesthetics, traditional Korean architecture is characterized by its simplicity, elegance, and understated beauty. Buildings are typically low-rise structures with tiled roofs, wooden beams, and paper-covered windows, reflecting a deep respect for tradition, and craftsmanship. Ornamentation is kept to a minimum, with emphasis placed on the natural beauty of materials, and the skillful execution of construction techniques. Traditional Korean architecture also makes use of symbolic motifs such as dragons, phoenixes, and lotus flowers, which carry cultural, and spiritual significance, and add meaning, and depth to the design.

The preservation, and promotion of traditional Korean architecture are essential for maintaining the cultural identity, and heritage of Korea. Through initiatives such as the Folk Village architecture, efforts are being made to safeguard these architectural treasures and pass them on to future generations. By studying, and appreciating traditional Korean architecture, we gain valuable insights into the history, culture, and values of the Korean people, and develop a greater appreciation for the beauty, and significance of these ancient structures.

Traditional Korean architecture is a testament to the creativity, ingenuity, and wisdom of the Korean people. The Folk Village architecture serves as a window into the past, allowing us to explore, and experience the rich architectural heritage of Korea. By preserving, studying, and celebrating traditional Korean architecture, we not only honor the achievements of our ancestors but also gain a deeper understanding of our own cultural roots, and traditions. Let us continue to cherish, and protect these architectural treasures for generations to come, ensuring that the beauty, and wisdom of traditional Korean architecture will endure for many years to come.

Influences on Korean Architecture

The architecture of Korea is strongly tied to the traditions, and philosophies that shaped Korean culture, and society. Perhaps no influence has been greater than that of Confucianism, which emphasized social harmony, hierarchy, and respect for tradition, and ancestors. These Confucian values are deeply embedded in Korean architectural forms, styles, and building practices over centuries.

By examining specific architectural features, and their cultural significances, we can gain a deeper understanding of how Confucianism permeated everyday life in historic Korea. Architecture both shapes and reflects the norms of a society. In Korea, architecture acted as physical expression of Confucian ideals. A close analysis of this relationship provides valuable insights into Korea's cultural past, and the long-term impacts of this influential school of thought. Let us begin our exploration by looking at some key Confucian concepts, and seeing how they informed Korean architectural design principles and techniques.

One of the fundamental tenets of Confucianism is respect for hierarchy and authority. This was reflected spatially through the hierarchical organization of buildings, construction methods, and palatial architecture reserved for royalty, and officials of high rank. Confucian scholar-officials held positions of respect, and power in Joseon dynasty Korea (1392-1910), acting as advisors to the king. Their social status was affirmed architecturally through large courtyard houses (hanok) with carefully arranged spaces denoting rank, and privilege.

Elite residences were constructed using quality materials like fine wooden beams, and floorboards covered in intricate inlaid geometric or floral patterns. Butted roof tiles, painted ceilings, and ornamental railings further enhanced the appearance of dignity and authority. In contrast, thatched peasants' homes, and buildings of lower standing utilized cheaper, humbler materials with plainer designs. Even the hierarchy of building components followed Confucian hierarchy - foundation stones topped gable ends, and roof ridges to physically demonstrate their support role.

A key organizing principle of Korean palatial architecture is the spirit wall (chorok) dividing inner palace quarters reserved for royalty from outer areas for officials, and servants. This stone wall represented an impassable boundary in both physical and social terms. Only the king (and at times the crown prince) could freely pass through it. Other elaborate elements reserved only for the highest ranks included throne halls, ornate courtyards, multi-tiered pagoda-style roof structures, and elaborately carved, and painted cornices, pillars, and ceiling brackets.

This hierarchical ordering of architectural spaces through a choice of materials, design, and division reflected the Confucian emphasis on social stratification and propriety. One's status in the socio-political hierarchy was literally set in architectural form - from the residences of officials, and commoners to the grand imperial palaces reserved exclusively for the king, and his family. Spatial arrangements demonstrated that all parts of society, from lowliest peasant to emperor, had clearly prescribed roles to play as part of a well-ordered whole.

Closely related to hierarchy is Confucian concern for order, and social harmony. Korean architecture expressed this value spatially through careful arrangement, and relationship of architectural components as well as overall site planning. Balance and symmetry were prized aesthetic qualities. Regular geometric shapes were favored - rectangles for platforms, and foundations, squares for columns, circles for pavilions, and roofs.

Patterns of repeated rectangular courtyard houses arranged around central open spaces, symbolic ornamentation, and ordered placement of building elements like woodwork carvings aimed to achieve tranquility through control of space. Even natural elements like rockwork, ponds, and greenery were precisely positioned for balance. This brought order from potential chaos, reflecting Confucian belief that societal order stems from each person occupying their proper place.

Harmony was also pursued through avoidance of excessive ornament or ostentatious features that might disrupt calm composition. Spatial relationships between buildings on a site were carefully regulated according to rules of propriety. Palaces followed symmetrical planning centered on a main axis, with ceremonial, and residential buildings arranged in neat rows backing formal gardens. This created serene atmosphere befitting governance according to Confucian ritual, and etiquette.

While incorporating symmetry, hierarchy, and geometry, Korean architecture strived for a natural simplicity inspired by Confucian respect for nature, and austerity. Plain tile or thatch roof lines blended harmoniously with surrounding natural scenery. Undecorated white-washed walls of hanok blended into their garden surroundings. Tall tapered roof ridges and deep eaves softened hard architectural edges, resembling natural hills or foliage.

Spaces were carefully integrated with the surrounding landscape through garden design that enhanced, rather than dominated nature. The design principle of "hwa-am-doh-gye" bringing scenery inside the house was fundamentally Confucian in characterizing human dwellings as residing harmoniously within the greater natural order. Architecture was meant to enhance nature's beauty rather than call attention to itself through excessive embellishment.

This can be seen in Confucian scholar's studios carefully situated with pleasing views of nearby gardens, mountains or streams. Even the simple hanok farms of peasants were thoughtfully planned as an extension of the surrounding rural environment rather than jarringly contrasting with it. Overall, Korean architecture pursued a quieter confidence through understated refinement and sensitivity to natural surroundings - expressing Confucian humility, and respect for nature's way. While affirming social hierarchy, it did so with minimal ostentation.

Reverence for ancestors constituted an important Confucian virtue, and one deeply engrained in Korean culture. This was manifested architecturally through ancestral shrines where tablets honoring family lineage were placed and regularly worshipped. Shrines took the form of thatched huts or purpose-built halls within larger village complexes or individual hanok compounds. Their design and location demonstrated filial piety.

Positioned upstream, and prominently near gate entrances, ancestral halls affirmed continuity of bloodlines. During Joseon period, it became expected for all yangban scholar-official families to maintain lineage records, and perform ancestor rites according to Confucian propriety. Ritual practices centered on arranged offerings of food, and drink presented before tablet altars accompanied by burning incense, and candles. Ceremonial architecture made sure this duty of intergenerational remembrance was afforded proper spatial recognition. Ancestral worship and lineage were so valorized it became a condition for holding public office.

Confucian emphasis on ritual practice and propriety was reflected in architecture through ceremonial buildings that hosted important seasonal, and life cycle rituals, and celebrations.

These included shrine halls, and pavilions for ancestor worship as well as main halls or platforms for events like weddings. Architectural design followed principles of ritual enactment.

For example, ceremonial spaces had highly regulated symmetrical layouts, symbolism in decorative motifs, and careful placement within overall sites according to guidelines of ritual purity, and directionality. The ritual mingling of inside, and outside was also pursued architecturally through design that intermixed interior, and exterior spaces without rigid boundary demarcation characteristic of Western houses.

Hanok, and other Korean structures utilized open courtyard arrangements to visually, and physically connect indoor, and outdoor living areas, enabling the harmonious flow of rituals, and daily activities interwoven throughout. This emphasis on indoor-outdoor permeability represented Confucian integration of ritual into everyday life according to cyclic seasons, and harmony with nature rather than compartmentalization.

Overall Korean architecture manifested Confucian spatial imperatives at various levels - from building typology, and arrangement of components to broader planning of palace complexes, and village sites according to principles of hierarchy, order, nature, and ritual interconnectedness of spaces. Confucian ideals were physically inscribed from macro to micro scale, representing a deep infusion of its social philosophies into Korea's architectural traditions over centuries. Though these traditions evolved with new influences like Buddhism, the underlying structuring around a Confucian worldview endured as an essential foundation of Korean architectural culture.

While Confucianism formed the ideological bedrock of Korean culture, another major influence arrived through the peaceful adoption of Buddhism in the 4th century AD. Originating from India, Buddhism spread throughout East Asia introducing novel concepts regarding the spiritual path, and nature of reality. These divergent perspectives progressively impacted Korea's traditional architectural customs. Buddhist temples saw creative experimentation infusing foreign styles within an existing Confucian-informed structural framework.

Over centuries, Korean Buddhist architecture developed a signature look blending imported elements with local techniques. Distinct from China or Japan, Korean styles bore clear fingerprints of their social context as the religion interacted with Confucian norms.

When Buddhism first permeated the Three Kingdoms period, initial converts were royalty eager to embrace novel cultural trends from afar. Buddhist concepts like emptiness, impermanence, and release from suffering proved alluring philosophical alternatives. Early wooden architecture adopted Indian-influenced styles of tall-roofed halls suitable for sermons, and meditation according to Buddhist ritual. Distinct from native Korean residences, religious buildings took rectilinear forms with bracketing throughout curved eaves.

Use of inner, and outer corridor arrangements provided spatial separation according to Indian modes. However, architects worked within limits - fire safety codes prohibited elaborate towering wooden structures prone to burning once common. Thus early Korean temples gravitated toward simpler single-winged designs of single halls surrounded by covered walkways, blending familiar layouts with foreign aesthetics. Buddhist concepts may have been novel, but architectural experimentation adapted such imports gradually through existing practical filters regarding construction materials, and styles fit for climatic conditions.

Once fired bricks became available in the 7th century, Buddhist construction found a more durable, and stable medium for artistic expression. Elegant multi-tiered brick pagodas arose, inspired by Indian stupas, and Chinese prototypes but uniquely Korean through subtle differences in proportion, decorative carving, and coloration. Complexes absorbed influences from Silla, Baekje, and Goguryeo Kingdom styles while obeying modular geometric planning ideals of Buddhist site design with gateways, sutra-storage buildings, and bells positioned according to ritual codes.

Symmetrical arrangements of Nampa Pavilion roofs expressed balance, and harmony as an ideal of existence according to Buddhist doctrine. Continued expansion saw mountain temple retreats built for ascetics, consciously integrating architectures within surrounding scenery. Natural stone provided rugged charm, and longevity for sculptures, lanterns, and pathways. Distinctive Korean folklore motifs carved into go board patterns acknowledged a continued synthesis of religious, and cultural forms.

During Goryeo, lavish five-story stone pagodas arose as one of the most iconic architectural symbols representing the kingdom's pride in offering patronage of Buddhism at grand scales. Though rooted in Indian inspirations, these Korean structures had their own character through stouter proportions, arching eaves with gracefully curved corners rather than sharp right angles of Chinese originals. Their stonework required a great reservoir of resources, and technical skills - a testament to faith's lofty position in society.

As Buddhism matured in Korea alongside Confucianism, distinct qualities of religious artistry emerged from temple sites selectively borrowing foreign forms but uniquely accentuating native tastes. Delicate elegance characterized by graceful tile, and shake steeples atop compact bases, eschewing heavier foreign architectures now. Organically blending human designs with scenic mountain backdrops featured tall pines, lush bamboo, and flowering apricot surrounding simple structures harmonized with nature according to Daoist-tinged ideals.

Porches and verandas blurred inside-outside divisions, dissolving boundaries amid lush environs. Intricate stone lanterns, pagodas, and effigies drew from Chinese calligraphy, folklore, and indigenous practices while retaining Korea's warm artistic palette imbued through coloured tiles, painted eaves, cinnamon woodwork, and vermilion walls. Uniquely ornate, and refined carvings into bamboo, blooms, and twisting vines adorned every surface according to special artistry. Such distinctive aesthetics embodied spiritually grounded artistic urges, well-matched for meditative monasteries.

Distinctive architectural trends also arose adjusting foreign forms sensitively to Confucian concepts of propriety, and hierarchy still valued by society. More modest temple town layouts replaced grandiose imported models but retained balanced, geometric arrangements for peace. Homes for contemplatives embraced simple nature, and austerity valued by Confucian sages as conducive to focus. Meanwhile royal patrons bestowed resources to construct artistic wonders like Seokguram, flawlessly balancing Buddhist symbolism, and grandeur within surrounding sublime landscapes.

Architectural exchanges between China, and the Three Kingdoms of ancient Korea began in earnest around the 4th century AD. Initial imports comprised woodworking styles from northern Chinese buildings emphasizing curved eaves supported by ornate bracketing systems. Braced structural frameworks enabled towering wooden halls suitable for Buddhist ceremonies carried by expanding religion. While adopted enthusiastically, Korean styles retained visual cues of native traditions like corner-levelling gangbeop through modulated bracketing extensions.

Simple pavilions arose for scholars in Chinese garden settings at royal courts, yetKorean adaptations utilized familiar design principles embedding such imported forms amid native garden conceptions favouring asymmetrical framing of landscapes. Architectural programs overall followed modular geometric planning gridded by gates, and boundary-markers according to Confucian, and Buddhist organizational precepts espoused by China. But fluid Korean styles united nature, and architecture through balanced indoor-outdoor flows of space seldom achieved to same degree in China.

Mastery of fired brick and granite construction allowed Korean temples and shrines to reach new monumental scales with imported multi-story pagoda, and temple styles. Lavish 5-storey Songak bulgung stone pagodas arose as regional treasures displaying technical virtuosity through arching curved eaves yet retaining subtle Korean proportions. In the 10th century Goryeo, techniques diffused enabling wood-covered brick structures boasting advanced solar design, and cross-structural bracketing.

While Chinese originals concentrated weight, versatile Korean architects maximized lightness through delicate curvature reminiscent of native wooden works. Artistically carved, and glazed bricks displayed intricate foliate patterns drawn from Chinese precedents yet uniquely styled. Painted earthenware wall tiles covered structures according to indigenous tastes favoring warm pastel tones inspired by nature.

Luxurious city palace compounds arose amid imported Chinese-style garden landscapes yet retained Korean penchant for simplicity blending constructed, and natural realms.

As Confucian scholars wrested royal control during Joseon dynasty amid frequent Chinese tributary missions, architectural interchange between the two most-prominent East Asian nations entered a golden age. Elaborate wooden palaces copied Chinese imperial models yet adapted for dignified mountain sites Korea favoured, balanced through indigenous design principles seeking harmony between buildings, and scenic terrain.

Complexes housed distinctive vermilion Korean-style buildings exhibiting carefully modulated bracketing systems anchoring curved tiled roofs balanced atop lofty white-washed walls. These anchored quadrangles of smaller pavilions for contemplation nestled amid wandering paths, ponds, and artistically framed vistas drawn from Chinese scholars' garden styles. Subtle botanical cues evoked the four seasons in Confucian fashion through flowerings selected by native taste.

Meanwhile at the imperial court in Seoul, palatial architecture concentrated authority within walled cities through multi-tiered wooden, and masonry buildings surmounted by ornate carved tiled roofs ascending skyward. These epic architectural feats showcased technical expertise through towering decorative elements yet retained balance through earthbound Korean aesthetics calming the eye through graded transitions between heavy foundations and soaring ridges. Splendors drew admiration from foreign envoys yet remained dignified through reserved refinement according finesse valued by Confucian scholars.

Over centuries, mutual borrowings generated uniquely Korean styles drawing from diversity of influences. Elegant five-rise pagodas blended Chinese symbolism into balanced architectural harmony according to Buddhist precepts through carefully elongated eaves soaring heavenwards yet anchored through wide sturdy bases. Subtly curved flying corners imparted a serene grace minimizing angularity common in Chinese originals. Vibrantly glazed roof tiles and dazzling sculptural details drawn from Song dynasty examples yet stylistically Korean.

Deeply recessed eaves supported by exquisitely carved brackets shaded walls enabling distinctive Korean surface art including vermilion, sky blue pigments, flower motifs, and symbolic guardian creatures blended with indigenous folkloric designs. Grand scale reflected royal magnificence yet boldness tempered through balanced restraint, and integrative siting harnessing surrounding terrain. Within this distinctive artistic language, Korean architecture cultivated its own identity negotiating varied cultural influences according to principles of simplicity, balance, and sensitive blending of constructed, and natural realms.

The early 20th century brought significant changes to the Korean peninsula as Imperial

Japan consolidated control through its colonial administration from 1910 to 1945. Alongside social, and political impacts, Korean architecture encountered new cross-cultural influences from the occupying force. Rejecting Korea's traditional aesthetic virtues with disdain, Japan imposed modernization programs systematically altering the built landscape.

While resistance arose, strategic cooptation of Korean talents also occurred. Hybrid architectural forms emerged negotiating indigenous styles and imported Japanese imperial styles. This era established patterns that infused contemporary Korean architecture with dualistic tensions between tradition, and modernity. By examining specific buildings, and planning initiatives, we gain insight into architecture's role navigating colonial rule as well as seeds planted for independent Korea's later creative evolution.

Upon annexation, Korean architecture faced radical transformation as Japan dismissed it as backwards. Traditional hanok courtyard homes were reviled as antiquated, and insular compared to fashionable Western, and Japanese contemporary styles. Systematic demolition and replacement programs targeted legacy structures for perceived health, and safety deficiencies according to imported modernist theories. Historic urban cores gave way to new street grids, and masonry buildings emulating Japanese imperial styles through grand scales, symmetry, and decorative neoclassical flourishes.

Institutional buildings arose through these pioneering reconstruction efforts including government halls, and railway stations crafted from stone, brick, and reinforced concrete. While innovative materials forged monumental statements of colonial progress, aesthetic guidelines enforced Japanese architectural fashion through reference to Shinto shrine styles alien to Korea. Early 20th century Seoul underwent jarring makeovers disrupting organic urban fabric developed over centuries in balance with Confucian precepts through harmonious placement amid flowing streams, and mountains which Japanese revisionists disparaged.

Despite early shocks, Korean talents mobilized creatively under changed circumstances. Notable architects like Jeong Dong-youn selectively integrated European techniques within rediscovered native design lineages through restored Gyeongbok palace blending traditional elegance with steel construction. Korean builders collaborated producing landmark hybrid structures like Deoksugung's fusion of traditional gardens, and ceremonial spaces within modern plazas, and buildings.

Simultaneously, hidden pockets of resistance upheld legacy through restored heritage sites, and clandestine preservation of architectural manual transcriptions. In the countryside, traditional village patterns endured less directly targeted. When properly valued, Korean ingenuity flourished within the colonial framework producing masterworks bridging eras. The Taj Mahal-inspired Seoul Station emerged from this syncretic spirit, juxtaposing Islamic-inspired domes, and arches amid Japanese stylistic elements balanced by open Korean planning embracing nature.

As Imperial Japan ramped up militarism in the 1930s, Korean architecture faced renewed assimilationist pressures. The colonial government stoked ultranationalist Shinto shrine construction as sites of imperial ideology forcing appropriation of Confucian sanctuaries. Simultaneously, rapid industrialization spawned new urban zones, and worker housing emphasizing efficiency, and density according to principles emphasizing social control through regulated standardization alien to Korean lived experiences.

While unlocking modern construction techniques, applied style remained alienating through rigid geometries rejecting balancing of nature. In countryside, agricultural collectivization dismantled traditional village orders. By 1943, the colonial government repealed kisaeng performance restrictions with geisha houses booming - altering social fabric. While introducing new building types, foreign impositions crudely supplanted indigenous architectural virtues honed over centuries reflecting lived realities of peninsula's varied communities. Wartime erosion of autonomy reached new extremes, yet seeds of distinctively Korean modernity persisted awaiting independence.

Liberation in 1945 released pent-up creativity as cultural institutions revived preserving traditional arts. The Democratic People's Republic established in the North rejected Western, and

Japanese imports developing Socialist Classicism through monumental buildings proclaiming self-reliance according to theories emphasizing direct connections with the populace. These retained balanced organization yet introduced foreign concepts through scale, and machismo disrupting prior harmonizing of construction with terrain.

Meanwhile, in Seoul, a construction boom fused reclaimed native patterns within modern idioms enabling masterworks blending traditional elegance, and contemporary functionality through restored Hanok districts, the Blue House, and bold new assemblies. internationally acclaimed architects emerged guided by pioneering spirit bridging past, and future through synthesized application of indigenous precepts to industrial means according flexible cultural imperatives. Forms gradually reasserted balance between man, and nature through modulated massings enlivened by vernacular surface textures.

Independent Korea explored innovative volumes sensitive to thermal performance yet anchored by lyrical refined details retaining essence of native architectural soul. International collaborations imported promising techniques while respecting indigenous rootedness. Ultimately a distinctive synthesis emerged negotiating cultural inheritance with aspirations of modern nationhood through creative adaptation.

The colonial period planted seeds for complexity defining contemporary Korean architecture's evolution negotiating imposition, and resistance, tradition versus modernity. While disruption jarred the built landscape, and social fabric, suppressed talents mobilized selectively coopting influences according vernacular virtues. Hybrid structures arose negotiating eras, establishing patterns of indigenized adaptation that shaped independent nation's confident assertion blending global techniques within balanced living practices honed over Korean history.

Monuments of the turbulent 20th century record architecture undertaking multifaceted role navigating colonial turbulence, and preserving cultural essence amid discontinuities. Revolutionary periods sprouted divergent interpretations according ideological differences, yet a common thread endured anchoring imagination through balance, refinement, and sensitive arrangement amid nature. Independent Korea's globally acclaimed architectural achievements flowered from this rich yet conflicted soil, grounding innovative expressions within enduring philosophical roots nurtured continuously despite ruptures. Ultimately tensions born of occupation stimulated creative dynamism defining Peninsula's contemporary architectural character and cultural confidence.

Modern Korean Architecture

Over the past century, rapid industrialization, and urbanization have transformed South Korea into one of Asia's most economically developed nations. Nowhere is this rapid transformation more visible than in Korea's skylines, filled with towering skyscrapers representing the country's ascent on the global stage. Once focused around low-rise traditional architecture, Korean cities have embraced ambitious height through sophisticated high-rises negotiating modern techniques with cultural roots.

By examining landmark projects, we gain insights into how Korean architects, and developers have pioneered new heights respecting indigenous principles of balance, material refinement, and sensitive integration of urban landscapes. Emerging trends also reveal deeper cultural undercurrents, with skyscrapers acting as symbolic vessels for national aspirations into a hi-tech future rooted in historical virtues.

Korea's early modern architecture following independence was dominated by austerity amid widespread rubble. However, groundbreaking projects in 1950s Seoul pointed to future ambitions. The 26-story Capitol building arose as Northeast Asia's tallest at the time through innovative braced frame construction. While advancing engineering, its curving forms echoed traditional Korean ceramic roof curves beautifully balanced.

Mecca-inspired Seoul Mosque blended Islamic domes with vernacular carved details, setting patterns of selective cultural fusion. Early superstructures negotiated conflicting desires for hi-tech novelty, and heritage preservation through modulated modernizations. High-rises gradually densified commercial districts yet retained human scales through podiums integrating plazas, and greenery according to biophilic design values. Subtle integrations of nature mitigated hard urbanism, upholding balance integral to cultural identity.

Seoul's skyline dramatically evolved through ambitious projects in subsequent decades cementing its status as a burgeoning "Asian tiger" economy. Grand complexes took hold including 63 Building famed for blending International Style with intricate low-relief ornamentation. Landmark towers arose like Koryo Fire, and Marine Headquarters' tapered spires capping tapering volumes celebrating both technical achievement and restrained elegance.

Yet greater heights awaited. The Korea World Trade Center punctuated the skyline in 1974 through 71 floors of curtain wall glass marrying international aesthetics with rising national confidence. Nearby towers manifested scaled-up traditional roof forms beautifully balanced atop narrow bases through proportions satisfying occidental ratios while retaining oriental refinements. High-tech additions like N-Tower introduced daring experiments in facade engineering, pushing design frontiers through cultural hybridity.

Developments accelerated alongside economic growth. In the late 1980s, the triumphal 150-meter Trade Tower arose celebrating open global trade through shimmering modernist grandeur. Despite rising scales, planners judiciously located imposing towers amid buffered open spaces, and pedestrian paths according to biophilic planning advocating humane density. Balance prevailed ensuring the dignified coexistence of nature, and new developments.

Entering the 21st century, Korean metropolises underwent explosive transformations with new financial districts, and vast mixed-use urban villages extending skyward. Landmark projects broke new height barriers representing the rising stature of Korean conglomerates on the global stage. The Northeast Asia's then-tallest Northeast Asia Trade Tower punctuated Seoul at over 250 meters in 1992.

Greater heights followed at a relentless pace. Lotte World Tower claimed Korea's pinnacle in 2017 through its 555-meter peak, and innovative engineering marrying technical prowess with restrained decorative virtuosity. Beyond grand statements, intricate podium designs activated plazas through integrated greenery, water features, and pedestrian networks modulating transitions between towering heights, and human scales below.

International projects also saw Korean imprints. In Dubai, the elite observation deck capped Burj

Khalifa leveraged Korean expertise with mastery of ambitious scales. Regardless of location, hallmarks of balanced massing, refined detailing, and integration of urban landscapes within towering volumes endured as architects negotiated shifting conditions with consistent cultural principles.

Several trends have defined contemporary Korean architecture at ambitious heights. Technical experimentation continues breaking records through projects optimizing wind resistance, seismic performance, and sky gardens according to environmental priorities. Sustainability increasingly factors as developments pursue LEED certification through features like triple-glazed insulating units optimized for thermal efficiency.

At the same time, subtler cultural inheritances endure. Modulated setbacks balance imposing scales with surrounding streetscapes. Shimmering aluminum and glass skins marry cutting-edge technologies with restrained surfaces celebrating craft through delicate patterns evoking traditional stone carving, and metalwork. Interiors prioritize biophilic qualities through abundant greenery, daylighting, and connection to nature. Cultural fusion remains evident too as developments embed Korean Hanok courtyard styles amid towering volumes.

Most strikingly, towering pinnacles often feature modulated tapering or elaborate spires distinctly Korean in refinement despite global vernaculars. Height appears attained through balanced increments according to philosophical imperatives of graduated transitions between grounded bases, and soaring peaks. Ambition transcends records through cultivated taste informed by centuries of cultural practice. Developments' scale amplifies while virtues endure, upholding continuity amid exponential change.

A pioneering modernist, Park established Korea's first architecture department at Seoul National University in the tumultuous postwar decades. Beyond seminal teaching, his restrained rationalist designs skillfully adapted international materials to indigenous tectonic principles through balanced massings emerged from organic proportions.

Landmarks included the elegant 1967 Seoul Court of Appeals integrating urban textures amid modulated massings bridging rootedness with modernity. Nature remained vital through planted podiums alleviating hard edges. Meanwhile Park Ju-yeon memorial library resurrected tradition through courtyard plans amid dynamic new volumes celebrating both legacy and potential through cultivated harmony. His moderate approach established patterns integrating global techniques respectfully within Korea's philosophical roots.

Recognized as Korea's foremost traditional architect, Kim devoted over 50 years to restoring and replicating heritage structures according to rigorous material analyses, and manual transcriptions. Beyond preservation, his original works ingeniously fused vernacular techniques within contemporary programs through inventive hybrids.

The seminal 1970 Daecheongbo pavilion combined thatched crowns with reinforced concrete vaulting marrying indigenous elegance with structural innovation. Recent clan halls, and hanok redevelopments in Seoul leverage refined heritage crafts according modern livability through inspired arrangement of spaces, and vistas. Sensitivity to patinaed textures and balanced flows of light imbue works globally with subtle cultural signatures rarely matched by foreign peers. Skilled application of vernacular wisdom endures as touchstone amid accelerating change.

Ascending into creative directorships, Kim navigated architectural development at national scales through groundbreaking urban planning and iconic buildings. The 1980s Central Government Complex in Daejeon established new standards blending modern functions within gracious public spaces, and surrounding woodland according to biophilic values.

Meanwhile project such as the sharp-edged Kangwon National University library introduced daring experimentation merging robust volumes with pixelated patterns embracing digitization through poised compositions. Later landmarks including KINTEX exhibition center extended such innovations elaborately articulating transitions between volumes to evoke flowing scenery through deft massing. Subtle but transformative works established Korea's growing confidence bridging digital modernity with cultural continuities.

One of Korea's most renowned contemporary architects, Park has spent decades reimagining urban environments on ambitious scales worldwide. The iconic 1986–1988 Dongdaemun Design Plaza regenerating historic districts melded cultural fusion adapting indigenous forms for a technology park bridging heritage, and future through balanced arrangements.

Beyond Korea, landmarks from Chiang Kai-shek Memorial Hall to Al Mamoura enhanced public realms according biophilic priorities moderating interactions between nature, architecture, and urban textures. Sustainable designs optimized thermal, and ecological performance selectively integrating vernacular aesthetics. Dynamic works manifest philosophy perceiving architecture as vessel cultivating humane urban experiences amid accelerating change through careful mediation of scales, spaces, and materials according enduring precepts.

Embodying new generations, Jang has ascended internationally through bold explorations of structural potentials within cultural groundings. The shimmering 2010 Suncheonman Museum stitches indigenous metalwork craft with avant-garde geometries celebrating technical finesse through restrained articulations of complex structural joinery.

Landmark projects from Gimhae Tower to public housing in Singapore transcend superficial mimicry by infusing alien materials with distinctive decorative motifs according vernacular metaphors, and symbolic patterns. Works manifest continuing evolution perceiving rising scales, and digital potentials as occasions to refurbish rather than discard cultural inheritance by cultivating refined expressions adaptable across frontiers. His hybrid vigor portends architecture's role shaping global dialogues with uniquely Korean character.

Through their pioneering works and philosophies, contemporary Korean architects have skillfully negotiated competing priorities of technological frontiers, ambitious scales, and cultural rootedness. From Park Jong-seon's patient integration of global techniques to Kim Swoo-geun's heritage restoration sophistication, and Jang Yeong-sil's structural explorations, each generation establishes patterns transplanting indigenous aesthetic principles to new mediums according to enduring values of balance, refinement, and nature.

Their groundbreaking projects have come to define Korea's built identity globally, establishing the nation as an innovator navigating modern transitions through selective adaptations anchored by philosophical centers undisturbed amid exponential change. Visions unite heritage, and future through harmony instead of opposition, perceiving growth as cultivated inwardly before manifesting outwardly on scales ever ampler. Architecture thus acts as vessel continually cultivating culture amid perpetual motion, lending works relevance enduring across eras.

As environmental awareness has grown globally, sustainable architecture establishing harmony between nature, and built forms has ascended in priority. Korean architects at the forefront of this movement negotiate humanity's increasing footprint through masterworks skillfully integrating greenhouse-reducing technologies, biophilic planning principles, and vernacular aesthetics within ambitious programs.

Emerging in tandem with rapid postwar development, these pioneers shaped a uniquely Korean approach synthesizing ancestral wisdoms, and novel techniques. Results establish the nation internationally as innovator navigating transitions judiciously through creative works balancing societal, ecological, and cultural imperatives.

Precursor projects surfaced amid reconstruction, anticipating later flourishing. In the 1960s Seongnam Apartments introduced solar design optimizing daylight, ventilation, and greenery according to biophilic precedents from traditional hanok organizing spaces. Groundbreaking for its time, the development established humane density patterns emulated globally through balanced arrangements enlivening surrounding landscapes.

In 1970, Kim Swoo-geun's pioneering Daecheongbo pavilion combined thatched roofs from vernacular precursors with reinforced concrete vaulting inaugurating experimentation in eco-material hybrids skillfully marrying heritage craftsmanship within sustainable innovations. These seeds nurtured later emergence of environmentally conscious architecture guided by balancing humanity's place amid natural contexts - a fundamentally Confucian worldview updated for present imperatives.

Leading exponents proliferated projects into the new millennium establishing Korea as vanguard. Kunsoo Park finessed biophilic urbanism elevating public life through works like the vertical recreation space-filled 2009 Suwon Tower. Meanwhile, James Kwak optimized thermal performance in masterworks as the sun-tracking Konyang University Graduate School through deft massings.

Jang Yeong-sil advances biomimetic approaches replicating indigenous metalworking techniques' structural resiliency, and shimmer through daring experimentation. His 2010 Suncheonman Museum seamlessly integrates regional forms, and materials with photovoltaics through balanced compositions anticipating living architecture's future. Landmark projects integrate indigenous virtues - proportion, refined craft, permeability, and situatedness within sustaining environs according ancestry's moderated utilization of nature.

Statutory bodies guide nationwide innovations respecting cultural wisdom. The Korean Green Building Council spearheads policy through standards certifying exemplary projects according indigenous precedents balancing built volumes, daylighting, ventilation, greenery, and energy performance. Their criteria recognize developments upholding balance, and resource efficiency without sacrificing graces honed by generations experience living alongside nature.

Large-scale residential, and commercial projects consistently rank among top worldwide green buildings credits. I'Park Hwaseong epitomizes achievements through vernacular-inspired compact clusters, photovoltaics, and LED lighting optimized for interactions between occupants, and surroundings. Militant posturing finds no place - ambitions expressed through judicious arrangements elevating quality of life according ingrained philosophies. National institutions nurture talents paving contemporary architecture's course through selective adaptation.

Through continued innovation, Korean architects pioneering sustainable designs skillfully navigate multiple imperatives according balanced cultural principles. Experimentation integrating ancestral wisdoms, and novel techniques synthesizes indigenous virtues attuned to planetary needs. Their masterworks skillfully mediate tensions informing humanity's role amid accelerating change - upholding graceful, egalitarian lifestyles through selective incorporation of means promoting resource efficiency, and reduced impact upon fragile ecologies.

By perceiving growth as inwardly cultivated harmonization rather than outward supremacy, contemporary Korean green architecture establishes nation as caring innovator through works globally renowned for balanced elevations of lived experience amid multiplying scales, and uncertainties. Sustainability advances through selective adaptations replenishing, and refurbishing inheritance, cultivating culture's spiritual center undisturbed despite transformations witnessed around. Architecture thus persists as vessel navigating transitions judiciously through creative coordination of built, and natural realms in service of coherence, rather than opposition, across generations.

Cultural, and Symbolic Meanings

The ancient Chinese philosophy of feng shui, meaning "wind-water", holds that harmonious positioning of buildings, and objects can positively influence the flows of vital energy or chi through surrounding landscapes. While native to China, feng shui principles resonated with Korea's analogous focus on balanced arrangements according to spiritual forces. Over generations, Korean architects organically fused such considerations into works renowned for sensitive integration within natural contexts.

Feng shui prioritized auspicious orientation aligned with chi's flows through cardinal directions as key determinants of good fortune. Similarly paramount in Korean architecture, buildings traditionally faced south towards sunlight while maintaining open northern exposures according to seasonal rhythms.

Gentle southern-facing slopes proved favored sites as chi could ascend unimpeded into compound cores. Meanwhile carefully calculated spatial arrangements channeled positive energies between enclosed interior courts open to skies through regulated apertures, and vista lines mimicking feng shui's "central streaming" principles. Considerations endured in modern designs like the intricate orientation, and arrangements modulating flows between interior, and exterior spaces at Lee Woon Yeol's refined Teheranroc residences.

Guardian figurines like stone military generals arranged in pairs flanking entrances according to Feng Shui's pairing of material forms safeguarded positive chi and deterred malign presences. Traditional Korean buildings similarly featured protective animal statues at gateways while placement of foundation stones represented spiritual role as earthly protector anchor.

Archways incorporated symbolic guardian images into balanced, often symmetrical formations conductive of nourishing currents according cosmological visions. Monumental instances emerged in regal architecture's lavish entryways balanced by decoratively carved mythological figures. Contemporary works creatively adapted these venerable functions through subtle forms - vibrant sculptures at gateways or strategic arrangement of boulders in works by Jang Yeong-sil.

Feng shui stressed buildings nestled amid auspicious landforms could bolster occupying family's prosperity, and security. Embracing hills, and valleys modulated chi's circulations usefully. Likewise Koreans intuitively sited constructions upon sloping terrain featuring flowing streams according to inherent preference for undulating topographies conductive of spiritual harmony.

Traditional villages naturally oriented around watercourses integrated into refined landscape compositions. Similarly modern projects attune constructions amid fluidscapes - Kunsoo Park expertly marries surging waterway, greenery, and angular volumes at Incheon's Riverwalk Apartments. Mastery threads fluid currents through rectilinear forms, upholding cultural lineage perceiving architecture's role cultivating flows amid dynamic environs. Subtle undercurrents thus infuse works with distinctive vitality.

While native to Chinese thought, such feng shui principles resonated profoundly with Korea's intuitive architectural wisdom balancing functionality, materiality, and delicate positioning amid landscapes according ancestral precepts. Their seepage occurred gradually through organic assimilation rather than direct import, synthesizing multiple cosmological lenses.

Today numerous landmark projects embed sophisticated fusion of techniques within balanced compositions subtly conducting positive forces. Whether guardian figures, auspicious orientations or sensitive flows between construction, and nature's dynamism, works capture the essence of perceiving humanity's role cultivating spiritual experience between land, and psyche. Architecture thereby emerges sustained vessel navigating modernity through selective adaptations replenishing cultural roots with insights enlivening inheritance from within for evolving contexts. Feng shui's fingerprints thus lend works relevance transcending eras through timeless coordination of built, and natural realms in tuned accord.

Ancestral structures celebrated regional uniqueness through warm earthy tones imbuing walls according vernacular aesthetics. Ochres, umbers, and subtle mineral pigments surfaced natural timber, stone, and thatch with harmonizing patinas aged beautifully by elements. Comparatively fine wooden architectural members showcased varied grains through selective oil staining.

Meanwhile, auspicious ceremonial architecture featured vivid accents. Vermilion gates and carved pillars married fiery orange-red hue with symbolic guardianship according ritual import. These balanced restrained timbers elsewhere in restorative neutral shades. Traditional palimpsests expertly layered tones graduated by proportion, and placement, from foundation colours deepest to crowning roof ridges heavensward glowing. Subtle gradients depicted nature's balanced ascent into mountains through refined transitions.

Postwar developments introduced novel materials marrying indigenous palettes. Clean yet diverse concrete finishes selectively integrated regional pigments within poured surfaces. Resulting in intricate patterning, terrazzo-emulated age-old stacked stonework, and tiled floors distinguished by place.

Emergent glass and metals prompted daring colours wed delicately. Structural frames featured indigos mimicking cascading foliage, and waterways, contrasting pale panes filled by verdant landscapes. Regional folkloric florals, and wildlife motifs adorned elevator doors, and window trims through digital printing according contemporary tastes. Dynamic coordination celebrated continuity amid transitions through selective revival anchoring modernity within cultural heritage refreshed from within.

Recent architectures explore environmental applications. Daylit atriums and curtain walls showcase optimized spectral properties through special photovoltaic glazings. Meanwhile complex double skins harvest natural ventilation according climate demands modulated by material combinations.

Internally, serene wooden interiors reinterpret heritage crafts through bespoke milling, and staining optimized for acoustic dampening, and wellbeing. Sustainably harvested pine, and maple manifest indigenous respect for living materials through aesthetic appreciation of graining according ancestry. Increasing green building credits see traditional tiles, bricks, and textiles integrated innovatively to lend works distinction according tactile associations carrying spiritual nourishment across generations.

Through selective adaptations of colors, textures, and tactile technologies anchored by rooted artistic sensibilities, Korean architecture's material identity maintains continuity amid transformation. Nature remains exemplar, as ancestral techniques judiciously integrate vibrant palettes within graded compositions conveying symbolic proportion, and connection to place. Contemporary works revive these virtues fostering cultural renewal from within through creative coordinations elevating lived experience.

Mythical beasts secured architectural thresholds emulating pastoral guardians against malign forces. Tigers, lions, and dragons carved fluidly into beams, and piers symbolized ancestral protection. Their graces endowed ceremonial buildings grandeur according ritual function. Guardians anchored constructions spiritually through balanced compositions imbuing welcoming portals with dignity.

Motifs proliferated subtly into modern entries. Sleek reflective guardian statues now stand sentry before corporate towers, government halls, and high-end residences maintaining ancestral auspices. Meanwhile exterior ceramic 'ghost-deterrents' endure warding spirits from redeveloped hanok districts testifying heritage continuity amid transformations. Motifs cultivated continuity through creative renewal anchored by philosophical tenets.

Floral, and botanical designs

Abundant floral patterning expressed Confucian ideals celebrating harmony amid diversity according seasonal rhythms. Delicate chrysanthemums, peonies, and orchids adorned walls, tiles, and wooden surfaces in balanced arrangements through standardized schematics. Their aesthetics evoked spiritual refreshment through intimate indoor-outdoor flows.

Contemporary designs revive heritage florae reinterpreting indigenous arrangements through intricately patterned resin inlay, moss-covered walls, and decorative metalworks. Modern conveniences embedding nature through intertwining botanical forms pay homage to ancestral wisdoms manifesting ongoing cultural regeneration from within through creative adaptations.

Rectilinear compositions symbolized cosmological balance according universal order. Repeating gridworks, gu patterns, and nesting squares organized plazas, and façades harmoniously. Tiles, and brick articulated geometry through pigments matching surrounding scenery.

Modern executions infuse glass curtain walls, and steel beams with subtle geometric accents inspired by tradition. Pixelated details reference ancient precedence in advanced materials to imbue towering volumes with cultural signatures internationally recognizable through selective revival anchored in philosophies transcending medium. Architecture thereby emerges sustained vessel mediating transitions judiciously.

Select material curators lend edifices distinguishing signatures internationally while respecting indigenous virtues. Their coordination establishes architecture's role navigating transitions replenishing rather than rupturing inheritance to cultivate spiritual coherence across frontiers, and epochs through balanced application of tones infused by deeper cosmological visions perceiving nature's vibrant tapestries as a source.

Preservation, and Restoration

As humanity's built, and natural treasures face increasing threats amid social disruptions, the UNESCO World Heritage program seeks to recognize and protect irreplaceable cultural sites representing outstanding achievements of humanity. Numerous architectural, and landscape sites within Korea today feature on this prestigious international register, a testament to their enduring value for all people.

By exploring several inscribed locations, we gain perspective on indigenous artistic, and planning traditions that shaped unique regional identities while imparting universal lessons. Sites connect humanity across frontiers through profound heritage nourishing collective spirit despite discontinuities. Their preservation sustains cultural viability through continuity cultivated from ancestral wisdom.

Declared in 2000, this ensemble represents an 8th century capital containing over 100 archaeological sites across 38 square kilometers. Ruins like Seokguram Grotto, and Bulguksa Temple complex showcase Silla Kingdom Buddhist architectural styles merging stone pavilions within mountain backdrops through balanced compositions.

Meanwhile the grass-covered Tumuli Park burial mounds offer rare insights into indigenous funeral rites. Their long-term archaeological conservation nurtures cultural understandings despite disruption. Refined techniques integrating monumentality amid natural contexts impart artistic imprints internationally relatable despite origins over 1000 years past. Their peaceful vision uplifts through nurturing ties uniting diverse populations across temporal barriers.

Inscribed in 2007, this site signifies Jeju Island's distinctive basalt rockscapes molded by volcanic eruptions into scenic tablelands, cliffs, and coastlines continuing dynamic creation. Intricate tube systems inside tuff cone mountains offer glimpses into Earth's formative processes while housing rare mineral clusters and underground pools.

Indigenous villagers adapted ingeniously upon this rugged yet biodiverse landscape through balancing pastoral livelihoods with reverence. Their sustainable traditions crafting sod roofings, and stone 'dol hareubangs' upon windswept vistas invite apprehending humankind amid dynamic contexts. Conservation perpetuates lessons perceiving humanity enlivened participating within greater natural orders greater.

Recognized in 2010, these mountain farming hamlets preserve 16th-17th century clan communities organized according to Confucian, and feng shui principles. Intricate clusters of thatched, and wood houses navigate terrain through balanced arrangements of ritual spaces, common areas, and defended villages.

Fieldstone walls, streams, and forests delineate organic residential zones. Living cultural practices sustain continuity through heritage tours, crafts, and seasonal rites. Their preservation fosters cultural resilience by nurturing understanding humanity's interconnectivity within dynamic contexts across epochs demonstrated through structural precedence adaptable to diversification amid alterations.

Inscribed in 2010, these hiking routes spread across Jeju Island's scenic pastures, seashores, and lava tube regions offer cultural pilgrimages through interactions between natural vistas, and tangible heritage. Over 300km of meandering trails marked by stone stacks, cairns, and wooden signage lead through working farms and fishing coves.

Their establishment empowered sustainable appreciation of natural treasures according ancestral norms balancing protection with utilization for prosperity. Reviving such earthbound spiritual journeys cultivates relations between humanity, and places nurturing responsibility across generations. Sites recognize both ecological riches and cultural practices manifesting humankind thoughtfully interwoven within sustaining environs.

Statutes from the 1960s designated significant cultural assets, and regulated alterations upon designated hanok villages, and palaces. Over 600 historic districts and individual structures now receive preservation orders maintained through skilled restoration artisans and the Cultural Heritage Administration orchestrating nationwide coordination.

Specialised training academies cultivate rare craft abilities unlocking technical insights enabling sympathetic reconstructions. Master carpenters cultivate refined joinery, and thatching reinvigorating structural longevity through selective nurturing. Simultaneously, the National Research Institute of Cultural Heritage harnesses scientific analyses deciphering material compositions, and degradation facilitating knowledge applications across continents.

Challenging natural formations necessitate ingenuity conserving volcanically molded Jeju landscapes amid intensifying tourism. The Jeju Heritage Foundation spearheads adaptive regeneration nurturing ecological heritage according indigenous precedent balancing utilization, and protection.

Reforestation programs reconstitute pine windbreaks while sod roof conservation projects harmonize atmospheric demands with architectural veracity to safeguard cultural continuity. Coastal management initiatives stabilize eroding lava cliffs through ecologically attuned fortification anchored by indigenous stonework mimicking rugged basalt textures. Balanced renewable utilization perpetuates spiritual enrichment by fostering understanding humanity's role amid dynamic systems in accord with ancestral norms.

Grassroots networks sustain continuity through heritage appreciation, and skills transfer organized locally yet nationally coordinated. The Hanok Conservation Centre enlivens redeveloped Seoul districts through community volunteerism restoring structures housing traditional performance troupes, and craftspeople.

Rural foundations revive dormant villages converting farmlands sensitively into experiential living museums. Traditional foods, crafts, and architecture perpetuate through participatory conservation cultivated by place, and inhabitants in ongoing reciprocity. Their initiatives foster cultural belonging through experience nurturing understanding humanity sustained through balanced relations between ancestors, inhabitants, and locale across generations.

While heritage conservation progresses judiciously through specialized techniques and community involvement, tensions inevitably arise negotiating ruptured histories, divergent perspectives, and modernization demands. Korean architecture restoration navigates complex realities through selective adaptations anchored culturally yet vulnerable amid accelerating change. Controversies surface valuable discussions illuminating balanced approaches addressing competing priorities respecting inheritance vitality.

Rapid reconstruction introduced disorienting alterations conflicting with traditional village aesthetics and social fabrics. Contention arose between heritage preservation ideals, and modernization pressures enabling accelerated density. Protections disrupted redevelopment profits yet unrestrained 'improvements' threatened spiritual nourishment.

Compromise emerged through selectively concentrated residential reconstruction amid preserved streetscapes, and common areas addressing multiple visions. Shared spaces fostered continuity through judicious integration of vernacular forms within planned urbanism moderating opposing outlooks. Cooperative initiatives cultivated understanding diverse outlooks remained reconcilable through balanced mediation nurturing rather than opposition.

Disputes emerged regarding reconstructed attributes' veracity amid technological evolution. While traditional methods unlocked structural secrets, replicate roofs, and tiles diverged materially from ancestral versions. Debates addressed whether modified imitations sustain ancestral vitality or become historical simulacra diluting inherence.

Nuanced positions appreciate both continuity and change's inevitability according to context. Selective revival anchors spiritual centers through balanced coordination preserving craft methods, and proportional arrangements despite material flux according to ecological realities and safety standards. Continual cultivation aspires coherence through selective adaptations anchored philosophically, uplifting through shared nourishment rather than absolutism.

Controversies arose regarding integrated international restoration specialists amid self-reliance aspirations. While outsourced expertise accelerated reconstruction, and craft apprenticeships, suspicions emerged foreigners prioritized opportunism over cultural sensitivity. Simultaneously local artisans faced preservation-trade conflicts amid full restoration specialization affecting livelihoods.

Cooperative solutions emerged pairing international specialists with local apprentices through long term placements cultivating cross cultural understanding integral to sensitive projects. Coordination affirmed indigenous wisdom directing works anchored philosophically through respecting craftspeople role as custodians according to ancestral responsibility. Multifaceted cooperation prioritized sharing across boundaries according to virtues of reciprocity, and nourishment over sectarianism.

Navigating restoration complexities demands nuanced mediation perceiving disputes not as ruptures but opportunities cultivating shared flourishing. Judicious coordination addresses competing visions through balanced adaptations anchored by philosophical centers undisturbed. Selective revival replenishes rather than severs inheritance by elevating inhabitation experience according to virtues sustaining cultural viability amid flux. Continual renewal cultivates spiritual coherence navigating transitions judiciously through care, understanding, and nourishment across differences. Architecture emerges sustained historical vessel navigating modernity guided by sensitivity to ancestral intentionality, and posterity's flourishing in accord.

Future of Korean Architecture

Humanity faces accelerating transformations through digitalization, climate change, and urbanization, architecture takes on expanded roles elevating lived experience through groundbreaking designs respecting cultural continuities. Pioneering Korean innovators negotiate ascending scales with technical mastery balanced respect for philosophical centers sustaining inherited virtues according to indigenous visions.

Appreciating nature's influence upon wellbeing, trends prioritize biophilic integration nurturing inhabitants' spiritual enrichment. Innovations optimize thermal comfort naturally through adaptive facades integrating phase-change materials controlling heatflux modulated by exterior conditions.

Digital controls coordinate dynamic shading, and openings connecting interiors with fluctuating landscapes. Greenery proliferates too through expansive skygardens, and living walls integrating ecosystems within built forms. Rigorous master planning situates constructions to retain vistas and absorb stormwater through rainscapes according indigenous precedents balancing urbanization amid sustaining environs. Works cultivate multi-sensory interactions elevating lived experience through judicious intertwinings of constructed, and natural realms elevating inhabited experience.

Novel fabrication marries inherited craft precision with mass-customizability. Advanced digitizing restores endangered techniques through virtual manual transcriptions enabling heritage restoration globally. Simultaneously, digitally molded surfaces resurrect subtle decorative patterns upon non-traditional substrates through programmed elastic deformations according indigenous schematics.

Artificial intelligence will personalize architectural styles synthesizing ancestral forms to habitats' unique contexts through balanced arrangements optimized for function, and nourishment. Robotics too will streamline complex assemblies while upholding refined details according to durable philosophies. Their synthesis elevates and sustains ancestral inheritances through selective applications nurturing spiritual coherence across transitions. Architecture emerges thereby fortified vessel navigating modernity judiciously through continuity cultivated interiorly.

Scalable offsite construction unlocks masterplanning potentials through structured yet adaptable modular volumes. Their standardized connections integrate sustainable prefabricated units optimized for durability, disassembly, and structural performance into high-density precincts respecting human scales.

Strategic arrangements distribute amenities according biophilic planning balancing communal, and private realms through outdoor activities, and green spaces enlivening surrounding landscapes. Integrated energy infrastructures harness solar, geothermal, and smart micro-grids according to ecological, and spatial priorities. Their synthesis elevates inhabitation merging global potentials judiciously through indigenous aesthetic sensibilities balancing density with nourishment according to virtues carrying inheritance across generations.

Early masters laid foundations skillfully modernizing according enduring precepts. Park Jong-seon balanced moderation transforming urban textures thoughtfully through restrained rationalism. His sensitive integrations of nature amid structures established patterns attracting global pupils, and praise establishing coherent patterns merging origins, and potentials.

Simultaneously abroad, talents amplified indigenous aesthetics to ambitious programs. Architectural Record lauded the Ministry of Health as a "quiet triumph" harmonizing monumentality within landscape amid 1950s Tokyo reconstruction. Their compositions showcased nuanced coordinations meriting emulation globally. Distinct signatures emerged through judicious nestings of rectilinears organically amid nature upholding philosophy elevating through balance.

As affluence grew, cultural cosmopolitanism expanded Koreans' clientele globally. Icons arose through selective fusion marrying technical prowess, refined compositions, and ancestral narratives identifiable across frontiers.

San Francisco's Korean Culture Centre juxtaposes rectilinears, and curvilinears recalling traditional ceramics balanced through carefully considered massings, and stonework textures according aesthetic virtues carrying inheritance distinctly. Experiential space flows marry global potentials judiciously through innate centeredness fortifying origins undimbed by alterations of place or conditions. Distinct signatures emerge sustained through selective adaptations anchored culturally.

In recent decades, proliferating publications featured Koreans' thoughtful innovations to challenging programs worldwide. Works garner accolades through balanced orchestrations moderating rising scales with sustaining elegance enriching inhabited experience.

Landmark projects grace magazine covers promoting sustainable mass timber across Europe, and Asia through judicious arrangements optimized for structural performance, craft, and spiritual nourishment. International design competitions honour nuanced negotiations between rectilinear, and nature through thoughtful massings balancing monumentality with intimacy according virtues preserving continuities across generations. Their acclaim reflects architecture's expanded significance navigating societal progress interiorly cultivated through selective adaptations fortifying ancestral tenets undimmed by transformations witnessed around.

Emerging platforms amplify Koreans' advocacy stewarding indigenous wisdom globally. Acclaimed theorists publish widely explicating subtle continuities embedded within technical explorations through international lectures, writings, and collaborative research nurturing cross cultural appreciation.

Simultaneously virtual transcriptions disseminate manual heritage teaching globally through digitizations reconciling origins, and potentials. Their stewardship recognizes architecture as sustained historical vessel navigating modernity through balanced coordinations interiorly replenishing rather than rupturing inheritance according to virtues imparting nourishment across epochs, and continents. Koreans thereby emerge guiders cultivating shared understanding, and flourishing through judicious heritage adaptations.

As computing power exponentially expands through innovations like augmented reality, 3D printing, robotics, and artificial intelligence, architecture's landscape undergoes profound shifts demanding judicious navigation. Korean masters rise to this challenge through groundbreaking works selectively coordinating promising techniques respectfully within indigenous philosophical centers fortifying cultural viability.

Computation streamlines concept development through parametric modeling, simulation, fabrication, and construction coordination.

Intricate massing studies optimize performance according rhythmic massing criteria articulating subtle transitions between nature, and volumes respecting biological precedent.

Simultaneously, BIM coordinations digitally prototype complex assemblies validating craft precision, and lifespan efficiency, and reducing material waste. Their balanced fusion fortifies inheritances refurbishing rather than supplanting according to virtues elevating despite societal accelerations. Simultaneously, VR reconstructs endangered sites internationally through manual transcriptions disseminating rare skills virtually as architectural memory.

Robotics transplant rare decorative techniques through programmed Elastic deformations resurrecting patterns according schematics upon novel substrates. Digital lutherie too programs complex joinery emulating structural finesse through calculated deformations optimized for structural integrity, and aesthetics.

Simultaneously robotics streamline assemblies while upholding craft values through regulated precision emulating biological systems efficaciously. Their judicious adaptations fortify origins by calibrating technical potentials interiorly through selective techniques preserving nuanced structural intentions defining cultural signatures according to philosophies undisturbed by societal innovations witnessed externally. Architecture emerges sustained vessel navigating transitions anchored philosophically through root virtues enriching inheritance for posterity.

Nature remains muse through biomimicry coordinating architectural behaviors upon shifting conditions. Adaptive building skins integrate phase change materials dynamically modulating openings, shading, and opacity balancing interior comfort with minimal energy consumption according seasonal cues.

Simultaneously biomimetic surfaces replicate structural, and insulating efficiencies of skins, feathers, and bark through intelligently layered enclosures optimized for insulation, and self-cleaning. Their orchestrations elevate inhabitation experience through judicious intertwinings of architectural functions, and sustaining environments according to virtues fortifying cultural continuity amid ascendant scales. Architecture emerges sustained historical preserver navigating modernity anchored innerly through wisdom cultivated across epochs.

Computation streamlines form studies yet outputs undergo nuanced vetting preserving virtues of balanced massing, tactility, and spatial flows according ancestral precedents. Outputs yield balanced volumes subtly articulating transitions between heights, and intimacy respecting biological precedent.

Simultaneously, digital mockups validate craft methods, and assemblies reviving complex joinery emulating structural finesse. Robotics assist artisans yet innovations meticulously emulate heirloom practitioners' regulated precision, and durability through programmed elastic formations. Their selective fusion replenishes origins by modulating technical means interiorly through rooted sensibilities undisturbed externally by proliferating alternatives.

Endangered techniques transplant through measured virtual recreations coupled with hands-on workshops globally. Simultaneously materials innovations judiciously substitute imperiled components to restore structural compositions, and proportional arrangements anchoring cultural identities.

3D modeling reconstructs manual transcriptions internationally preserving vanishing skills while catalyzing tactile appreciation. Augmented tutorials overlay schematics upon works enhancing experiential learning according living wisdoms. Their balanced coordination elevates heritage accessibility elevating spiritual nourishment through selective appropriations interiorly directed by philosophical centers undimmed.

Biomimicry coordinates architectural functions, and environs referencing nature's cue as living exemplar. Adaptive skins judiciously integrate phase changing materials to optimize occupant comfort through dynamic fenestration according natural metabolisms.

Simultaneously biomimetic forms replicate structural efficiencies of skins, feathers, and bark through novel assemblies optimized for insulation, self-repair, and modulated interior environmental conditions. Their orchestrations harmonize construction judiciously within sustaining surroundings according principles fortifying cultural continuity through selective applications from within directing outward potentials.

Through judicious coordinations balanced interiorly yet amplified outwardly, Korean architects establish technical means as cultural vessels navigating societal ascents anchored philosophically. Innovations judiciously enrich origins by modulating potentials to actualize virtues defining inheritances across fluctuating contexts. Heritage expressions emerge thereby sustained through selective renovations fortifying origins replenished from within as architecture emerges preserved guiding progress anchored by virtues imparting nourishment universally through care, understanding, and balance amid accelerating change witnessed around.

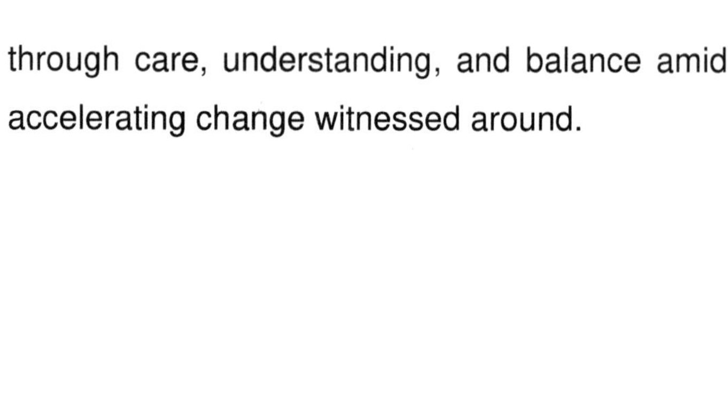

Disclaimer

The information contained in this book is for general informational purposes only. All information in this book is provided in good faith, however we make no representation or warranty of any kind, express or implied, regarding the accuracy, adequacy, validity, reliability, availability or completeness of any information in this book.

Under no circumstance shall the authors or publishers be held liable for any loss or damage of any kind incurred as a result of the use of the information included in this book. Your use of this information is at your own risk.

The views, and opinions expressed in this book are the author's own and do not necessarily reflect those of any affiliated organizations, companies, or governments.

While best efforts were used in preparing this book, the author makes no representations or warranties of any kind, and assumes no liabilities of any kind with respect to the accuracy or completeness of the contents, and specifically disclaims any implied warranties of merchantability or fitness of use for a particular purpose.

This book contains general information about architecture. The information is not advice, and should not be treated as such. The contents of this book are not intended to substitute for architectural, construction or engineering advice. If expert assistance is required, the services of a competent professional should be sought.

About the authors

Asem Al-Wasli (Arabic:عاصم الواصلي) is a Yemeni Musician, Author, and Writer.

Fuad Al-Qrize (Arabic:فؤاد الكريزي) is a Yemeni Musician, Producer, Author, and Writer, The chief executive officer (CEO) of Al-Qrize Productions.

Maher Asaad Baker (In Arabic: ماهر أسعد بكر), is a Syrian Musician, Author, and Journalist. He was born in Damascus, Syria in 1977.